Weekly Reader Books presents

# The Nitty-gritty of Family Life

A Children's Book about Living in a Family

by

## Joy Wilt

Illustrated by Ernie Hergenroeder

Educational Products Division
Word, Incorporated
Waco, Texas

# Author

JOY WILT is creator and director of Children's Ministries, an organization that provides resources "for people who care about children"—speakers, workshops, demonstrations, consulting services, and training institutes. A certified elementary school teacher, administrator, and early childhood specialist, Joy is also consultant to and professor in the master's degree program in children's ministries for Fuller Theological Seminary. Joy is a graduate of LaVerne College, LaVerne, California (B.A. in Biological Science), and Pacific Oaks College, Pasadena, California (M.A. in Human Development). She is author of three books, *Happily Ever After, An Uncomplicated Guide to Becoming a Superparent*, and *Taming the Big Bad Wolves*, as well as the popular *Can-Make-And-Do Books*. Joy's commitment "never to forget what it feels like to be a child" permeates the many innovative programs she has developed and her work as lecturer, consultant, writer, and—not least—mother of two children, Christopher and Lisa.

# Artist

ERNIE HERGENROEDER is founder and owner of Hergie & Associates (a visual communications studio and advertising agency). With the establishment of this company in 1975, "Hergie" and his wife, Faith, settled in San Jose with their four children, Lynn, Kathy, Stephen, and Beth. Active in community and church affairs, Hergie is involved in presenting creative workshops for teachers, ministers, and others who wish to understand the techniques of communicating visually. He also lectures in high schools to encourage young artists toward a career in commercial art. Hergie serves as a consultant to organizations such as the Police Athletic League (PAL), Girl Scouts, and religious and secular corporations. His ultimate goal is to touch the hearts of kids (8 to 80) all over the world—visually!

**This book is a presentation of Weekly Reader Books.**
**Weekly Reader Books offers book clubs for children from**
**preschool through junior high school.**

**For further information write to:**
**WEEKLY READER BOOKS**
**1250 Fairwood Ave.**
**Columbus, Ohio 43216**

The Nitty-gritty of Family Life

6 7 8 9 / 86 85 84

# Contents

# Introduction

The Nitty-gritty of Family Life is one of a series of books.    The complete set is called *Ready-Set-Grow!*

The Nitty-gritty of Family Life deals with the child as a member of a family and can be used by itself or as part of a program that utilizes all of the *Ready-Set-Grow!* books.

The Nitty-gritty of Family Life is specifically designed so that children can either read the book themselves or have it read to them.  This can be done at home, church, or school.  When reading to children, it is not necessary to complete the book at one sitting.  Concern should be given to the attention span of the individual child and his or her comprehension of the subject matter.

The Nitty-gritty of Family Life is designed to involve the child in the concepts that are being taught.  This is done by simply and carefully explaining each concept and then asking questions that invite a response from the child.  It is hoped that by answering the questions the child will personalize the concept and, thus, integrate it into his or her thinking.

The Nitty-gritty of Family Life defines the word family as "a group of people (two or more) who are related to each other and share the same home." The book helps the child understand his or her role as a member of a family.

Family relationships, rules, and responsibilities are all a part of family life. The Nitty-gritty of Family Life gives the following guidelines:

> establish healthy relationships with other family members,
>
> accept rules as a vital part of family life, and
>
> share responsibilities (if family life is to run smoothly, every family member must do his or her part.)

The Nitty-gritty of Family Life is designed to give the child a better understanding of his or her role as member of a family.

The Nitty-gritty of Family Life

You are a part of a family.

Your family is special, just as every other family is special.

No two families are exactly alike.
Every family is different.

Families come in different colors.

13

**Families come in different sizes.**

**Some families are small.**

Some families are large.

**Families come in different ages.**

**Some families are young.**

Some families are old.

This is a family.

This is a family.

This is a family.

This is a family.

This is a family.

A family is two or more people who are related to each other and often share the same home.

Some families live in houses.

Some families live in mobile homes.

Some families live in apartments.

Some families live on farms.

What is your family like?

How many people are in your family?

_____

What are their names and ages?

_____

_____

_____

Where does your family live?

_____

_____

# Chapter 1

# Family Roles

When a man has or adopts a child, he becomes a father.

When a woman has or adopts a child, she becomes a mother.

Every boy is his father and mother's son.

**If there are other children in a boy's family, he is their brother.**

**Every girl is her father and mother's daughter.**

34

If there are other children in a girl's family, she is their sister.

MARY IS MY SISTER.

A father's father is a grandfather.

A father's mother is a grandmother.

**A mother's father is a grandfather.**

**A mother's mother is a grandmother.**

**A father's brother is an uncle.**

A father's sister is an aunt.

SUSIE IS MY SISTER.

THIS IS OUR AUNT
SUSIE.

**A mother's brother is an uncle.**

**A mother's sister is an aunt.**

MARILYN IS MY SISTER.

THIS IS OUR
AUNT MARILYN.

**An uncle and aunt's children are cousins.**

Father, mother, brother(s), and sister(s)
are called the immediate family.

Grandparents, uncles, aunts, and cousins are called the extended family.

Who is in your immediate family?

_____

_____

_____

Who is in your extended family?

_____

_____

_____

_____

_____

Are you a brother?

Are you a sister?

Are you an uncle?

Are you an aunt?

Are you a cousin?

# Chapter 2

# Family Relationships

When two people are around each other a lot, they sometimes have disagreements and fights.

Sometimes a mother and father disagree and fight with each other.

Sometimes a parent and child disagree and fight with each other.

Sometimes a child disagrees and fights with a brother or sister.

It is normal for people who are together a lot to have disagreements and fights.

Disagreements and fights can often be good.

They can allow people to express their anger, frustration, and other feelings that may be upsetting them.

They can allow people to get problems out in the open and hopefully solve them.

Family disagreements and fights can often be helpful if family members remember these three things.

Family members should be honest with each other. They should tell each other the truth about what is happening, and what they think and feel about the situation.

Family members should not harm each other.

Family members should love, respect, and trust each other.

Family disagreements and fights are an important part of family relationships.

**Cooperation is also an important part of family relationships.**

It is very important that family members cooperate and help each other learn and grow.

**Support is also an important part of family relationships.**

61

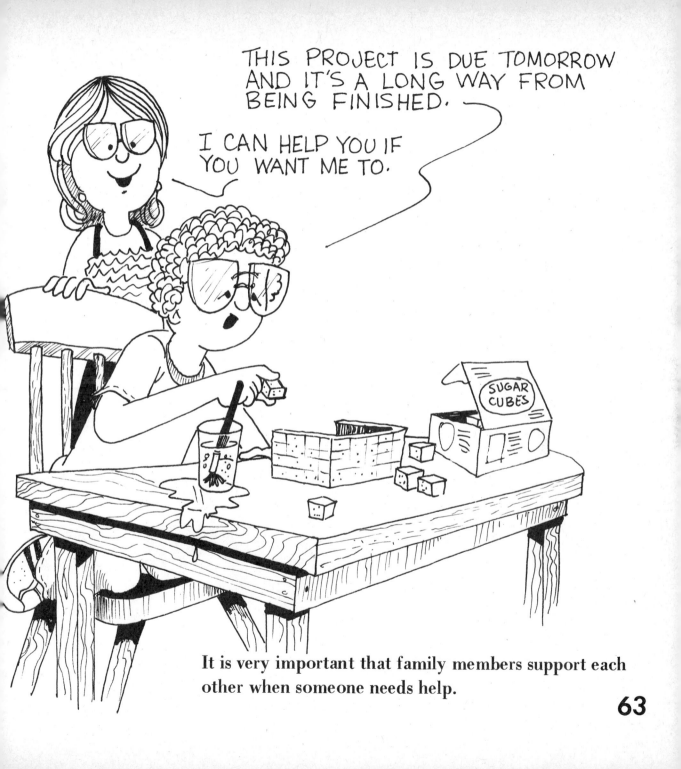

It is very important that family members support each other when someone needs help.

**Sharing is also an important part of family relationships.**

It is very important that family members share their things with each other.

Remember.

Family disagreements and fights can often be helpful if family members

> are honest with each other;
>
> do not harm each other; and
>
> love, respect, and trust each other.

Family relationships will be better if family members
      cooperate with each other,
      support each other, and
      share with each other.

How are your relationships with the people in your family?

When you disagree and fight, are you honest? ☒ Yes ☐ No

Do you try not to harm each other? ☐ Yes ☒ No

Do you love, respect, and trust each other? ☑ Yes ☐ No

Do you cooperate with the people in your family? ☒ Yes ☐ No

Do you support them? ☒ Yes ☐ No

Do you share your things with them? ☒ Yes ☐ NO

# Chapter 3

# Family Rules

Wherever there are two or more people, it is important to have rules.

Rules are guidelines that tell people how to act and what to do.

Every family has rules. Some rules are talked about and agreed upon by everyone in the family. These are called spoken rules. Here is an example of a spoken rule.

Other rules may not be talked about and agreed upon, but everyone in the family knows that they exist. These rules are called unspoken rules. Here is an example of an unspoken rule.

Spoken rules are oftentimes more effective than unspoken ones. When a spoken rule is made, everyone has a chance to talk about the rule and make sure he or she understands it. But when a rule is not talked over by the family members, sometimes it can be misunderstood. Whether a rule is spoken or unspoken, it needs to be respected and followed equally by every member of the family.

Because every family is different, every family has a different set of rules. Each family must make a set of rules that fits its particular situation.

When a family makes a set of rules, it should be remembered that rules work best when everyone who has to obey them helps make the rules.

It is important for families to have rules about space.

Rules about space tell family members

> what areas in and around the home are OK to be in,
>
> what areas in and around the home are off limits,
>
> what activities can and cannot be done in certain areas, and
>
> where family members can and cannot go when they leave home.

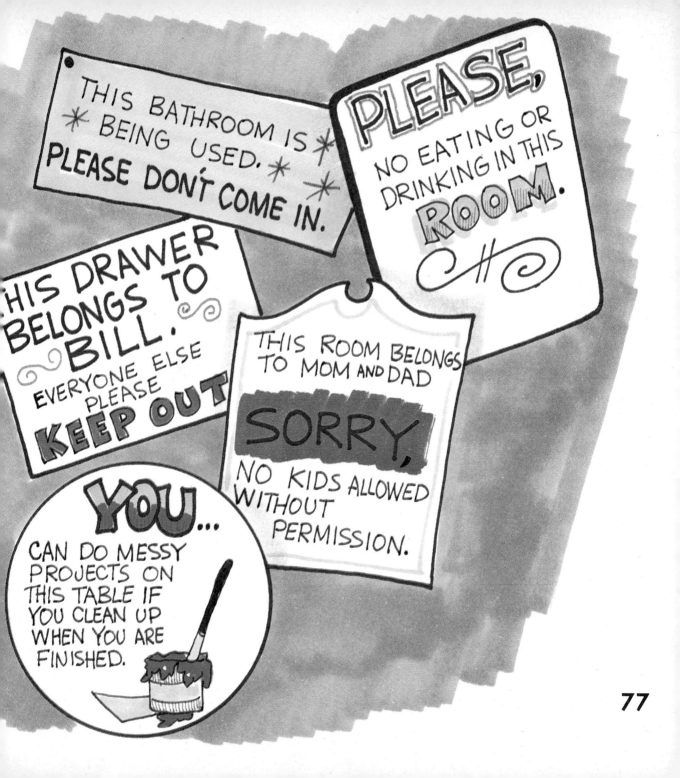

77

**What are your family's rules about space?**

**What areas in and around your home are OK for you to be in?**

my Room Bathroo upstairs Living Room

**What areas in and around your home are off limits to you?**

marinahas Room

In what areas are you allowed to eat?

_Kicthen_

Are there any areas where you are not allowed to eat?

_every were els than_

In what areas are you allowed to make a mess?

___

Are there any areas where you are not allowed to make a mess?

___

In what areas can you play?

___

Are there any areas where you are not allowed to play?

___

Where are you allowed to go when you leave home?

___

Are there any places you aren't allowed to go?

___

It is important for families to have rules about time.

Rules about time tell family members

>when things happen (the family schedule),

>when certain things should be finished, and

>when things can and cannot be done at certain times.

81

**What are your family rules about time?**

**Do you have special times when you eat your meals?** ☐ ☐
**Yes** **No**

**When do you eat breakfast?**_____

**When do you eat lunch?**_____

**When do you eat dinner?**_____

**When do you have to be home in the evening?**_____

**When is your bedtime?**_____

Are there other times when you or your family do certain things? ☐ ☐
Yes No

If there are, use this chart to list some of
those times and what activities are done then.

| TIME | ACTIVITY |
|------|----------|
|      |          |
|      |          |
|      |          |
|      |          |

It is important for families to have rules about possessions.

Rules about possessions tell family members

> what each person owns,

> what owners can and cannot do with their things,

> how to borrow and return things, and

> what must be done when someone's things are lost, abused, or broken by another family member.

84

What are your family's rules about possessions?



What are some of the things you own?

_____


_____

What are you allowed to do with the things you own?

_____

What are you not allowed to do with the things you own?

_____

If you want to borrow something from another family member,
what do you have to do?

_____

If someone should lose, abuse, or break your things, what would happen?

_____

If you should lose, abuse, or break someone else's things, what would happen?

_____

It is important for families to have rules about work.

Rules about work tell family members

who is supposed to work,

what work needs to be done,

when the work needs to be done, and

where the work needs to be done.

| FAMILY WORK CHART | | |
|---|---|---|
| Name | Job to be done | When the job is to be done |
| Bill | Empty the trash | Every Tuesday and Thursday |
| | Dry the dishes | Every other week |
| | Set the table | Every other week |
| | Make his bed and clean his room | Every day |
| | Mow the lawn and weed the garden | Every other Saturday |
| | Vacuum and dust the house | Every other Saturday |
| Mary | Feed the dog and cat | Every day |
| | Dry the dishes | Every other week |
| | Set the table | Every other week |
| | Make her bed and clean her room | Every day |
| | Mow the lawn and weed the garden | Every other Saturday |
| | Vacuum and dust the house | Every other Saturday |

What are your family's rules about work?

Make a work chart for your family.

| Name | Job to be done |
|------|----------------|
| | |

FAMIL

**ORK CHART**

When the job is to be done

It is important for families to have rules about play.

Rules about play tell family members

who is OK to play with,

what is healthy and safe to play with,

when it is healthy and safe to play, and

where it is healthy and safe to play.

93

What are your family's rules about play?


Who are some of the people it is good for you to play with?

_____

Who are some of the people you shouldn't play with?

_____

What are some of the things that are healthy and safe to play with?

_____

What are some of the things you shouldn't play with?

_____

When is it healthy and safe for you to play?

_____

When shouldn't you play?

_____

Where is it healthy and safe for you to play?

_____

Where shouldn't you play?

_____

It is important for families to have rules about habits and customs.

Rules about habits and customs tell family members

what they will do during time spent together;

what they will do for vacations, holidays, and special events;

how often certain practices will be repeated; and

how the family will choose to act or behave.

What are your family's rules about habits and customs?

Did your family have a vacation together this year?  ☐ ☒
                                                      Yes  No

What did you do?

_____

List some of the holidays your family celebrates together.

_____

_____

List other special events that happen in your family.

_____

_____

Does your whole family ever get together during the day?  ☑ Yes  ☐ No

If so, what does your family do then?

_____

Are there special times set aside when your family does certain things?  ☑ Yes  ☐ No

List some things your family chooses to do again and again.

_____

_____

99

It is important for families to have rules.

Some rules are spoken while others are unspoken.

Whether a rule is spoken or unspoken, it is important that it be respected and followed by every member of the family.

Every family has its own set of rules about

      space,
      time,
      possessions,
      work,
      play, and
      habits and customs.

# Chapter 4

# Family Responsibilities

Wherever there are two or more people, there are always jobs that have to be done.

Jobs are often called responsibilities.

103

It is not fair for one person in any family to take all of the responsibility and do every job that needs to be done. It is not good for the person who is doing everything, and it is not good for the people who are letting that person do everything.

If a family is to be healthy and happy, everyone must take some responsibility. Everyone must work so that no one person is doing everything.

Food, clothes, and a place to live cost money.

Someone has to earn money for the family to use.

All the things that a family uses need to be purchased.

MOM, I THINK I NEED SOME NEW SHOES.

Someone has to shop for the things that the family needs.

Things that the family buys must be paid for.

Someone has to pay the money that the family owes.

In order to live, people in the family need to eat.

Someone has to prepare the food for the family to eat. **109**

When people live in a home, it gets dirty and messy.

Someone has to organize and clean the place where the family lives.

When people wear clothing, it gets dirty too.
Someone has to wash and dry the clothes that the family wears.

Things that are used by the family sometimes break or stop working. Someone has to repair the things that break or stop working.

Some families live in homes where there are jobs to be done outside.

Someone has to do the work on the lawn and the outside of the house to keep them in good shape.

Some families own a car.

Someone has to clean, wash, and take care of the car.

There are babies and/or young children in some families.

Someone has to take care of the babies and small children in a family.

Some families have a pet.

Someone has to take care of the family pet.

Wherever there are families, there will always be garbage and trash.

Someone has to take care of the garbage and trash.

These are just a few of the responsibilities that families have. In every family there are a lot of jobs that need to be done.

A family can be healthy and happy if everyone remembers these two things.

Family members should always try to "share the load." Each person should take some responsibility and do his or her part to help the family out.

Family members should always try to appreciate one another for the things each person does.

Who earns the money that your family uses?

_____

Who shops for the things that your family needs?

_____

Who pays the money that your family owes?  (Who pays the bills?)

_____

Who prepares the food that your family eats?

_____

Who organizes and cleans the place where your family lives?

_____

Who washes and dries the clothes that your family wears?

_____

Who repairs the things that break or stop working?

_____

Who does the work on the lawn and the outside of the house?

_____

Who cleans, washes, and takes care of the car?

_____

Who takes care of the babies and small children in your family?

_____

Who takes care of your family's pet?

_____

Who takes care of the garbage and trash?

_____

What are some of your responsibilities? What are some of the jobs you do to help your family? _____

_____

Do you remember to appreciate and say thank-you to the other people in your family who are doing things to help out? ☒   ☐
                                                      Yes   No

# Conclusion

It is true that families do not stay the same forever.

Sometimes new members are added to families.

Children grow up and move away.

People grow old and die.

124

But families go on and on.

As long as there are people, there will be families:

Families where people laugh, cry, work, play, and grow together;
Families where people fight and then make up;
Families where people share and help each other out.

Being part of a family isn't always easy. There are

roles that have to be fulfilled,
relationships that have to be developed,
rules that have to be obeyed, and
responsibilities that have to be done.

But that's what life is all about. These things are all a part of living, growing, and . . .

The nitty-gritty of family life.